THE
WEST HIGHLAND
WHITE TERRIER

THE
WEST HIGHLAND
WHITE TERRIER

THE
WEST HIGHLAND
WHITE TERRIER

THE
WEST HIGHLAND
WHITE TERRIER

HOLLAND BUCKLEY

Foreword by John T. Ward

SMITHMARK

This edition published in 1998 by SMITHMARK Publishers, a division of U.S. Media Holdings, Inc., 115 West 18th Street, New York, NY 10011.

SMITHMARK books are available for bulk purchase for sales promotion or premium use. For details write or call the manager of special sales, SMITHMARK Publishers, 115 West 18th Street, New York, NY 10011; 212-519-1300.

ISBN: 0-7651-0811-9

Printed in China

10 9 8 7 6 5 4 3 2 1

Cover design: Hotfoot Studio

Library of Congress Cataloging-in-Publication Data

Buckley, Holland.
   The West Highland white terrier/ by Holland Buckley.
      p.   cm.
   Originally published: London: Illustatrated Kennel News Co. Ltd., 1911.
      ISBN 0-7651-0811-9 (alk. paper)
      1. West Highland white terrier.   I. Title.
   SF429.W4B835   1998   98-3902
   636.755--dc21   CIP

Dedicated to the COUNTESS OF ABERDEEN, now and for many years one of the bulwarks of the breed. A fast and strenuous friend to the little Highlander from the West Highlands of Scotland.

HER EXCELLENCY THE COUNTESS OF ABERDEEN.

FOREWORD

I can still remember my delight when I first found a copy of *The West Highland White Terrier*, a monograph by Holland Buckley. It was thirty years ago and it was one of only three copies of the original book I have ever seen.

Holland Buckley played an early and important role in the preservation of this wonderful breed. In the ninety years since he wrote this book, the breed has evolved and changed to some degree, and attitudes toward trimming are different. Yet, the wonderful West Highland White Terrier has, in essence, changed very little.

In his preface, Buckley writes, "To insist upon the type, general activity and character of the Highlander *par excellence* of Scottish breeds is everyone's duty . . . ." If his book encouraged breeders to protect the integrity of the breed, he said, "I shall have done a part to keep the pure West Highland Terrier from being the sport and victim of those [who would "improve" it]. Buckley's chapter on breeding is a classic, and should be required reading for all breeders. His list of breeding Don'ts could have been written yesterday.

This book is loaded with little gems of knowledge of interest to all Westie breeders and enthusiasts.

John T. Ward, 1998

Photo.] [*T. Fall, Baker Street.*

Mr. Holland Buckley.

THE WEST HIGHLAND WHITE TERRIER.

PREFACE

THE tremendous vogue that this fascinating terrier has attained—not only in the land of his making and adoption, but in America and many parts of the Continent, and our Colonies —makes it imperative that a standard work should be written to sustain and increase the immense popularity of our game little favourites.

To insist upon the type, general activity and character, of the Highlander *par excellence* of Scottish breeds is everyone's duty who is interested, and if, by a strenuous front being shown to the expressed desire of new fanciers and backsliders for Scottish terrier type, I shall have done a part to keep the pure West Highland terrier from being the sport and victim of those improvers (save the mark !) this work will not have been written in vain.

The watchwords of all breeders and exhibitors should be no alteration in type or character, and absolutely no trimming. One of the great charms of the breed to the ordinary person is that the exhibits are, in the main, shown absolutely natural, and not only look all the better for it but are better for being allowed to retain nature's covering against bleak and bitter weather.

Personally, when I am the adjudicator, I turn down without the slightest hesitation trimmed specimens.

There is another fine argument in favour of non-trimming, for by the universal adoption of this rule no one is penalised, all exhibitors are on a dead level, and true sport is assured.

HOLLAND BUCKLEY.

July 1*st*, 1911.

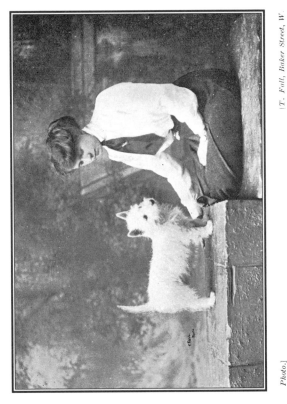

Mrs. Cecil Clare and Maulden Glisna.

Photo.]   [T. Fall, Baker Street, W.

MR. W. BAKER, HON. SECRETARY OF THE WEST
HIGHLAND WHITE TERRIER CLUB.

INTRODUCTION.

INTRODUCTION

THE chorus of almost unanimous vituperation with which the breed was greeted, upon its first introduction to the show bench, disheartened many of the breed's godfathers, but others made of sterner stuff plodded on, and met a reward long overdue, by the adoption of a standard of points and the establishment of specialist clubs to foster the breed, and recognition by the ruling body under the euphonic and widely embracing name of the West Highland White Terrier.

A popularity was immediately theirs which never would have been possible had the name of " Roseneath," Poltalloch, Cairn or White Scottish Terrier been persisted with.

We have not, however, escaped the crazes which have been so prolific in "improving" and finally ruining other breeds. Certainly the most dangerous attack, which, happily was repulsed with some slaughter, was the dictum that the " whites " must have a Scottie head, on a short Scottie back, and many specimens were benched, and for a time were successful in winning the majority of prizes, that were not only a travesty of their own breed but a libel on the grand breed they were supposed to represent *in white.* The public, however, who are in the long run the finest judges of all, whether it be sport, horses or dogs, never would stand the monstrosities alleged to be white Scottish terriers. So the little band of enthusiasts, who stuck so pluckily to their guns had the infinite pleasure of back marking the slap dash *improvers;* and of seeing their favourites, who were true in type and correct in weight, head the prize lists at the principal exhibitions.

That the breed's progress was greatly retarded by the craze admits of little doubt, but out of the evil great good came, as the weak-kneed, who, alas, are always with us, were greatly strengthened, and the Scottie type received very little commendation from the best judges.

The next craze that died a hard death was the insistence upon absolute straight fronts

Photo.]   [W. Illingworth, Northampton.
Mrs. M. S. Hunter and Morova and Newton Mora.

combined with lowness to ground, but the sight of the creatures paddling along, with their legs right under them, with their "little Marys" bumping the unkindly earth, was too much for the risible faculties of the Fancy and so another craze was killed by well-deserved ridicule.

That the present day admirers suffer for the sins of the faddists of bygone days is certain. Especially in the constant reversion to a foreign type and colour, so puzzling to the novice breeder, who will often slang well known stud dogs for begetting faults, which in all probability arise from the back blood of their own bitches.

That the breed has advanced enormously in all-round general excellence is a safe proposition which a walk round the benches of the great joint show will prove to demonstration.

We have no great prepotent dog like "Champion Morven," and now, alas, no great show dog resembling "Champion Kiltie," a brace of terriers, in the writer's judgment, fit to battle with the best of any breed ; for high quality and terrier character "Champion

Oronsay " was yet another wonderful terrier little, if any, inferior to the above-named.

The breed doubtless owe a well of gratitude to the owner of the last-named terrier, for in the Countess of Aberdeen it found its chief pillar, who made great and endless sacrifices for its advancement.

Although the historical side of any breed must appeal with great force both to the old hand and the novice, the writer's main endeavour will be in this book to render assistance to the novice who, after all, is the scientific breeder of to-morrow. If the lessons learned and digested are of the avail that are the main purposes of this book, my experience of many years of owning and breeding these fascinating little terriers will have carried, mayhap, the breeder nearer to the budding ambition of the true fancier's heart, which is the winning of the Challenge Cup at the Great Club Show in June, the greatest show for " Whites " of the year, where the entries are truly amazing in quality, and of plethoric proportions numerically.

The Hon. Mrs. Lascelles with a Grand Group.

Photo.]   [*Yates, Sheffield.*

Mr. William E. Gray.

HISTORY.

HISTORY.

Unlike most breeds of dogs of long descent, the back history of the White Highlander is fairly well known. Indeed, Colonel Malcolm of Poltalloch claimed by an attenuated chain of reasoning (which, although picturesque and vivid enough to the neophyte, scarcely carried conviction to the student) that the Scottish terrier owes its existing type to the influence of outside blood, and that the original terrier was actually of the type of the West Highlander.

The British Museum can profitably be visited by the careful student who will there, by poring over the National manuscripts, receive abundant evidence of the antiquity of the breed.

The writer has not only seen papers in Versailles but pictures of the Cairn terriers at work, which bore the imprint of the time of Louis the Great, and these Cairn terriers were identical in every way with a modern

West Highlander, with the exception that some were prick-eared and others drop-eared or semi-erect.

The point of long and distinguished ancestry being settled, mingled respect and admiration for the hardy breeder, who by insistence on working qualities and killing power, in the game little Skye, Poltalloch, Cairn, or West Highlander White, (call them what you will they are all merged into the latter now), must be the feeling of all who own sport in their compositions.

The name that would spring from any breeder's lips on being asked which is the dog that has had the greatest influence would of course be " Champion Morven." By reason of this terrier's super excellence as a show dog very many admirers were attracted to the breed, but in these pages we are more concerned with his undoubted prepotent power of stamping his descendants with his great individuality, gameness, and other correct show points.

" Brogach," " Morven's " sire, was a biggish

MR. W. PRENTICE'S BARLAE SNOWBALL.

ATHOLL, WHO OWNS THE MOST PERFECT BODY.

terrier with great bone and substance generally ; moderate in colour and long enough in
back, a point wherein the dam of "Morven"
excelled, for "Callaig" would, even in these
days, be described as of the medium length
with grand ribs. "Callaig," in alliance with
the afore-mentioned "Brogach," proved the
value of the stream of prepotent blood lines
by begetting a large number of terriers, some
merely plausible, but others both from a
bench point of view and considered from
future value of their blood, had done much,
indeed invaluable service, in fixing type and
shape in their descendants.

"Morven" stands alone, absolutely alone,
with his inborn faculty of begetting great
sons and daughters, who between them have
not only fixed the character, but the weight,
shape, and size of our present day front
rankers.

When the *Libro de Oro*, the Stud Book of
the breed comes to be written, it will be
obvious to the meanest understanding what
an immense power for good this great dog

has been in all that goes for superlative terrier type and formation.

I cannot remember at the moment whether "Champion Kiltie" ever did get his head in front of his great contemporary. In the ring, he was mostly I think, *proxime accessit*, but he never for a moment challenged the former's supremacy at Stud. For as great a bencher as "Kiltie" proved himself on many interesting occasions, he assuredly has not helped the breed by founding a great line of sons and daughters to perpetuate his many grand qualities.

His expatriation, therefore, to America, for the sum of £400 (*on dit*), while removing a great figure from our show benches, was little loss from the breeding point of view. This is all the more extraordinary as the number of bitches that visited him must have been enormous.

If I were asked to name the greatest dog or bitch I should unhesitatingly go for the charming "Runag," who is to-day the model of what a West Highlander should be in make,

Mrs. A. Henry Higginson and her West Highland
Terrier Ch. Dazzler Sands.

shape, and character. Her sire " Conar " was a prolific getter of average stock, but nothing else approaching that superlative specimen.

The only one that I can recall would, I think, be the Edinburgh champion, " Nevis," but as she happened to be my own property, I may of course be prejudiced in her favour. Unquestionably the best bodied dog ever benched was " Atholl," who proved his great character by siring " Glenmohr Model," whose first appearance at the Great Joint Show in 1910 was sensational. The Judge, Mr. B. W. Powlett, who is the happy possessor of ripe judgment, and also utterly fearless in its expression, put " Model " at the head of some of the strongest classes ever seen. That no judicial blunder was committed was proven in double quick time, for this rare little terrier qualified for his final challenge prize at the Crystal Palace within five months. Our American cousins with their usual indomitable pluck, again talked dollars, so " Model " joined " Kiltie," and " Dazzler Sands " in the United States.

LYNDHURST TINY AND JEAN.

INVERAILORT ROY.

The craze for white colours effectively put paid to the pretensions of " Atholl " to challenge honours, although in all other respects he was a very perfect terrier. To show what a tremendous pity a slavish adherence is to a point that in the old days never did form part in the *tout ensemble* of the breed, the above named " Atholl " was rarely used except by a few knowledgeable persons on his native heath, who soon reaped a splendid reward for their cuteness, for in double quick time, " Champion Glenmohr Model," "Champion Pure Gem," "Lothian Marvel," and a number of lesser lights were produced.

It does not take a vastly vivid imagination to picture the array of bench champions that this grand little chap would have sired had he been a champion himself. Owners of the Highlanders are, I am sorry to believe, just as sheeplike as those who " follow on," in other breeds.

" Atholl " who like his father " Champion Morven " is a dominant sire, and if great good looks are of the value that we generally assert

" Champion Glenmohr Model " is almost a " snip " to reproduce the dominant stream of blood that goes to make up his pedigree. One might here note the interesting—I had almost written the vital fact—that dogs that are truly made, with big well-sprung ribs, and powerful hind-quarters, are rarely over weight. " Brogach," the sire of " Morven," was 17 lbs. weight, " Atholl," Morven's best son, 16 lbs. " Model " the best great grandson of Brogach, 16 lbs.

The last named were splendidly proportioned and faced one with a look and expression implying great power in small compass. Certainly our American friends are lucky in their generation, for in " Model " they possess probably the most dominant stud force in the world.

" Ballach Bhan " sired a number of first class dogs and bitches, chief amongst whom would be " Inverailort Roy," whom I first saw at Birmingham, where he won the challenge prize. I thought him pretty lucky on that occasion, but had to eat my opinion at the

Kennel Club show last October where I gave him reserve champion. Bar his rather light coloured eyes, he is a grand sort, and may carry the " Ballach Bhan " line of blood to a successful consummation.

If I had to name the dog that should be selected to carry the " Morven " line, to breed truest to type and weight, I should, without hesitation, choose " Swaites Gaisgeach," who with (the pity of it) limited opportunities, has sired " Swaites Saighdear," " Swaites Spar," " Swaites Coll," " Swaites Jura," " Swaites Cuchullin," and " Lord Clyde." " Gaisgeach " is, I happen to know, a splendid worker with either fox or badger, and his descendants are all his way of thinking and tireless in manifesting it. " Morar " is another instance of the dominant line of blood, for in alliance with " Dudswell Jura," he got " Dazzler Sands," " Sparkler Sands," and can claim to have sired Mrs. M. Hunter's beautiful matron, " Newtonmore," the dam of some of our best terriers.

MRS. PHILIP BIRKIN WITH BLANTYRE MINNIE
AND BLANTYRE FLORA.

Photo.]   [Sport and General, London.

MRS LOGAN'S CHAMPION RUNAG.

MR. JOHN LEE'S MAULDEN CROFTER.

BREEDING.

BREEDING.

The making of a leading kennel of any breed is assuredly not a matter of luck or of scientific flair.

To possess a knowledge of all the back blood of the breed is not the royal road to the breeding of champion show stock, but the knowledge possessed of the failings and excellencies of the ancestry of our favourites must be of paramount importance in the selection of both sire and dam.

Many will assert that the proper application of Mendelian laws to our breeding operations automatically rule out of court a strict adherence to most well-practised rules of breeding show stock; but no amount of power to assimilate Mendel's theories, and ability to translate them into practice, will abolish the stern necessity of a figure system, wherein each figure represents and denotes much, very much, more than a mere unit, but which should indubitably mean dominancy in certain points which we wish to reproduce.

Just as it is an axiom that a fault once reproduced will take generation after generation to breed out, so it is just as certain that virtues originally bred for will long outlast even the ignorant mating best calculated to destroy the very virtues carefully built up.

The aim and object of every breeder should be, first and foremost, type and correct formation. What we desire to obtain, as lovers of the breed, are West Highland terriers, not merely a terrier with a short back and a white colour. We must first strike for the true type of the breed, and bring our purely fancy points in afterwards.

Character, and their adaptability for the work—for which the pioneers of the breed evolved them—should come next, and herein bodily formation is of the most crucial importance.

The accumulation of evidence of back blood influence is absolutely conclusive. The sensible breeder will accept the scientific evidence and be far on the road to breeding champions, while the scoffer is employing valuable time in producing wasters.

Supposing our keen breeder knows what he desires ; to produce the ideal West Highlander in his eye, as well as in actuality, he must possess some knowledge of the basic laws that govern breeding. The most urgent of these I take to be heredity. The breeder, whether observant or not, will sooner or later sit down and take notice of this tremendous influence.

My own records prove that the sire and dam contribute one-half of every attribute inherited, one quarter being placed to each parent. The four grandparents are responsible for one-fourth or separately one-sixteenth each. The eight great-grandparents are responsible in the descent to the extent of one-eighth, and so on. Of all the bequeathing to the offspring, variations will and do occur, but the above can be relied upon as a fair average. Prepotency is another remarkable power possessed by some dogs in the strain, of stamping their immediate characteristics, with either superlative excel-

Mrs. Logan and Groncach.

lencies, or the reverse. The importance of the number system is here again made manifest, so that the prepotent sire or dam may be ear-marked for future breeders. I recall that my little dog, " Champion Clonmel Cream o' the Skies " (he got his full title in the United States), always stamped through the generation his ideal eyes and ears, just as easily as I can remember that the dam of another of my best dogs used her prepotency to stamp the devil that was in her to her numerous descendants.

Right down foolish mating is the direct cause of half or two-thirds of the failures ; it has over-stocked the country with runts of the worst description.

The insensate rush of ever coming breeders to the fashionable sire, is the direct cause of this, just as if the first desire of the breeder is to breed pedigree stock, regardless of the suit-ability, or otherwise, of the sire pitched upon.

So, very many are merely driftwood, with no goal fixed in their mind's eye, and no mental picture of what they are striving for.

Even when the painstaking breeder has

recognised the importance of prepotency and heredity, atavism will not improbably upset his breeding theories by its undoubted power and great tendency to throw back to the ancestral line.

The great point to be grasped is that the embryo champion is the offspring of the whole line of ancestors from the full generations.

Consequently, no breed has suffered more from inbreeding than the Highlander in the old days, and not so very long ago it was almost impossible to handle these terriers in the ring without getting bitten. Out of a big collection at a Championship Show where I was adjudicating, only half-a-dozen properly stood up to be judged and handled. That was, however, before the present West Highland Club was formed, and I have no doubt at all that that fine organization has proved of splendid educational value in this as well as other respects.

A long course of inbreeding is bound to spell mental and bodily degeneration. Impotent dogs and hopelessly barren bitches, wasty puny pups, and mental idiots, are the surest penalties that follow ; but I am far from the opinion that inbreeding judiciously practised is harmful. The intense prepotency of some of the strains (other than the breed under notice) of my own kennel amply prove that inbreeding rationally carried out is all for the standardization of the variety.

In choosing the stud dog for your prospective litter, do not rush blindly to the great bench winner, who may himself be one of those extraordinary sports or flukes, which are the marvel of the ages ; or indeed do not heedlessly go to the other extreme, in its way just as fatal, and assume that any dog in your own kennel, if of fashionable pedigree, " will do the trick " as well. Remember that the sweets of owning great kennels never will or can be the portion of the slap dash brigade. All, or nearly all, owners of stud dogs are very human, and invariably by word painting make up the deficiencies of these world beaters, by the limning in of the ideal. A few " Don'ts " here would perhaps not be out of place.

Don't be behindhand in asking for advice from those qualified to give it.

Don't wait until your matron is ready for the visit, have the suitable sire in your mind and above all see that he is typical.

Don't fall to the lure of the owner of the cheap stud dog, what is cheap is generally nasty ; a litter that nobody wants, yourself included, is bound to be costly.

Don't allow your bitch to get hoglike in proportions, and then slang the stud dog for failure.

Don't fail to call to mind that the dog you select should resemble your bitch as nearly as possible in contour, and if he is superlative in those points wherein she is deficient so much more successful will the alliance be. See that he be healthy, a proved stockgetter, and not with a " flash " reputation.

The period of heat is readily recognised by the coloured discharge from the vagina. The changing condition of the vagina and the automatic stopping of the discharge are nature's warning of the true time of mating. I am often

Photo.]   [*T. Fall, Baker Street, W.*

CHAWSTON GARRY K.C.S.B. 382 P.

Photo.]   [*T. Fall, Baker Street, W.*

CHAWSTON GLENGARRY K.C.S.B. 2929.

knocked off my perch by the frequent display of astonishing ignorance of owners. Bitches often arrive when not in season at all; others appear when in the last stage and are almost impossible to have served.

Remember that it is far preferable to be too soon than too late. The company of the owner would be welcome to the bitch, and pleasurable to the owner of the stud dog, whenever possible.

The time of the dam may be calculated to expire on the sixty-third day after service, during the first part of this period, a life of natural freedom, plenty of good raw beef, and the latter part, steady exercise on the roads. Her food should, in these days, consist of lean meat, plenty of big bones, and phosphate of lime. The last six days the meat may be lessened, and rice, Quaker Oats, with occasional doses of olive oil, in fact a little of this rubbed on her stomach and vagina will immensely assist parturition.

As she becomes heavy take her with you on lead, and encourage any of your household to give her a friendly lead to the butcher or baker. For all the interest you can cram into her life the pups will not improbably pay you back tenfold.

It is of great importance that the bitch should be quite *au fait* with her surroundings, and she should be introduced to her whelping kennel at least nine days before she is due to whelp. I recommend a boarded floor and a straw bed, and on the last two days she should be given oatmeal gruel, and after parturition as well. Sheep's head broth, thickened with oatmeal, bread and gravy, or fresh milk should be her diet for quite three days, after which, supposing that everything is *couleur de rose*, anything wholesome may be given.

The pups being now on the high road to vigorous life, and granted that they are healthy, they should be left severely alone, until the lapping stage arrives, which should invariably be under a month's age. If at all possible let the milk be warm from the cow, and strengthened by one of the suitable preparations now on the market ; do not trouble in the least about solid foods, they are infinitely the better without them.

The old " swank " that milk breeds worms, I take no stock in at all. I know that it helps bone, health, and constitution.

The essentials to perfect success in breeding are unquestionably liberty, cleanliness, constant attention and feeding, and common-sense in the management of all four. To quote one of the most brainy and successful breeders of all times : " To attain continued success needs patience and endurance, and the optimistic temperament of *never ending hope*."

If I have done a small part in moulding the future of this fascinating breed by writing this contribution to the literature concerning the West Highlander I shall be proud, and beg, in conclusion, the privilege of quoting the eloquent peroration of the breed's first author and firm defender. " So breed them hardy, and breed them game, that they may ever uphold the reputation of their ancient home, the West Highlands of Scotland."

Photo.]   [*Blake & Edgar, Bedford.*

Mr. John Lee.

DESCRIPTION AND POINTS.

MR B. W. POWLETT.

DESCRIPTION AND POINTS.

Description and standard of points, as adopted by the West Highland White Terrier Club, are here given, with a few alterations which I think are desirable, and which shall be named.

The club's scale of points I have discarded as worthless and, indeed, ridiculous. I don't know who was responsible for the drawing up of the scale, but I am quite confident that the present skipper of the club is guiltless.

To start off with the egregious assumption that the general appearance is worthless in value sufficiently damns the scale, for the general appearance of the dog is the breed, shows the breed, and is so typical, showing class, power, characteristics, keenness, and distinction. All this is allotted 5 points. After that, one is not unduly staggered to find that colour is worth 10, and neck, 7½. Ye gods! neck 7½, as against the *tout ensemble* of the dog.

I have deleted from the description that the roof of the mouth should be black. I have, I suppose, judged every first class specimen, both before and after the club was instituted, and I have never yet seen any but parti-colour roofs in the best specimens, and honestly, I don't desire to ; there may be æsthetic reasons for the black hue to the "Thames Tunnel," but I know of no practical ones in the dogs, so have left that portion out as misleading.

In the description, No. 2, Colour, etc.,I have put that in, although I am by no means in agreement.

All things being equal, if I happen to be on the Woolsack, the " pure white " would naturally win against an inferior dog of the objectionable colour.

But give me the last-named, with a pull on the "pure one" in other points, and the "objection-able one " would be top dog in my ring, anyway.

We may one day breed them mostly white, but when, as now, the giants of the breed (heaven save the mark) are cream coloured, it savours of the worst hypocrisy to pretend that they are to be " outed "; because the rank and file of the Fancy find the game impossible to follow, and are in the same frame of mind as the beery individual who "Dunno' where 'e are."

CHAMPION LAGAVULIN.

HIELAN LASSIE.

The club weights I also disagree with. The ideal weights are, or should be, from my point of view: for bitches, 14 lbs. to 15 lbs; for dogs, 16 lbs. to 17 lbs. maximum.

A bitch who weighed but 12 lbs. would be a toy. To an old parliamentary hand this craze for points, which at one time I found not unamusing, I find now pathetic. Points! points! always first, and the dog afterwards, and the dog the sufferer all the time. The point judge operator will spend the best part of his time in the ring looking for points. The wily exhibitor will assist to his full, the dog may be a cringing, crawling, nervy beast, but his tail is put up, his feet placed fair and firm, and the rest of him being up to the standard, he runs out a winner.

There are no points for the gay *debonair* carriage, and "dauntless courage gleaming out of the keen eyes." For dash and urgent courage and terrier flair only receive 5 points, tucked under general appearance, for a slavish follower of the standard to adhere to.

STANDARD OF POINTS AS ADOPTED BY THE WEST HIGHLAND WHITE TERRIER CLUB OF ENGLAND.

No. 1. *The General Appearance* of the West Highland White Terrier is that of a small, game, hardy-looking Terrier, possessed with no small amount of self-esteem, with a varminty appearance, strongly built, deep in chest and back ribs, straight back and powerful quarters on muscular legs, and exhibiting in a marked degree a great combination of strength and activity. The coat should be about 2¼ inches long, white in colour, hard, with plenty of soft undercoat with no tendency to wave or curl. The tail should be as straight as possible and carried not too gaily, and covered with hard hair, but not bushy. The skull should not be too broad, being in proportion to the powerful jaws. The ears shall be as small and sharp-pointed as possible, and carried tightly up, and must be absolutely erect. The eyes of moderate size, dark hazel in colour, widely placed, with a sharp, bright, intelligent expression. The muzzle should not be too long, powerful, and gradually tapering towards the nose. The nose, roof of mouth, and pads of feet distinctly black in colour.

Mr. W. E. Gray's Padraig K.C.S.B. 355 P.

Mr. W. E. Gray's Ardmore.

No. 2. *Colour.*—Pure white; any other colour objectionable.

No. 3. *Coat.*—Very important, and seldom seen to perfection; must be double-coated. The outer coat consists of hard hair, about 2 inches long, and free from any curl. The under coat, which resembles fur, is short, soft and close. Open coats are objectionable.

No. 4. *Size.*—Dogs to weigh from 14 to 18 lbs., and Bitches from 12 to 16 lbs., and measure from 8 to 12 inches at the shoulder.

No. 5. *Skull.*—Should not be too narrow, being in proportion to his powerful jaw, not too long, slightly domed, and gradually tapering to the eyes, between which there should be a slight indentation or stop, eyebrows heavy, head and neck thickly coated with hair.

No. 6. *Eyes.*—Widely set apart, medium in size, dark hazel in colour, slightly sunk in the head, sharp and intelligent, which looking from under the heavy eyebrows give a piercing look. Full eyes and also light coloured eyes are very objectionable.

No. 7. *Muzzle.*—Should be nearly equal in length to the rest of the skull, powerful and gradually tapering towards the nose, which should be fairly wide. The jaws level and powerful, the teeth square or evenly met, well set and large for the size of the dog. The nose should be distinctly black in colour.

No. 8. *Ears.*—Small, erect, carried lightly up, and terminating in a sharp point. The hair of them should be short, smooth (velvety), and they should not be cut. The ears should be free from any fringe at the top. Round pointed, broad, and large ears are very objectionable, also ears too heavily covered with hair.

No. 9. *Neck.*—Muscular and nicely set on sloping shoulders.

No. 10. *Chest.*—Very deep, with breadth in proportion to the size of the dog.

No. 11. *Body.*—Compact, straight back, ribs deep and well arched in the upper half of ribs, presenting a flatish side appearance, loins broad and strong, hindquarters strong, muscular and wide across the top.

No. 12 *Legs and Feet.*—Both fore and hind legs should be short and muscular. The shoulder-blades should be comparatively broad, and well sloped backwards. The points of the shoulder-blades should be closely knitted into the backbone, so that very little movement of them should be noticeable when the dog is walking. The elbow should be close in to the body both when moving or standing, thus causing the fore leg to be well placed in under the shoulder. The fore legs should be straight and thickly covered with short hard hair. The hind legs should be short and sinewy. The thighs very muscular and not too wide apart.

Photo.]

[*T. Fall, Baker Street, W.*

GROUP OF PRIZEWINNERS AT MRS. CAMERON HEAD'S KENNELS.

The hocks bent and well set in under the body, so as to be fairly close to each other either when standing, walking, or trotting. The fore feet are larger than the hind ones, are round, proportionate in size, strong, thickly padded, and covered with short hard hair. The hind feet are smaller and thickly padded. The under surface of the pads of feet and all the nails should be distinctly black in colour. Cow hocks detract from the general appearance. Straight or weak hocks, both kinds, are undesirable, and should be guarded against.

No. 13. *Tail.*—Five or six inches long, covered with hard hairs, no feather, as straight as possible, carried gaily, but not curled over back. A long tail is objectionable. On no account should tails be docked, *vide* K.C. Rule VI. Appendix II.

No. 14. *Movement.*—Should be free, straight and easy all round. In front the leg should be freely extended forward by the shoulder. The hind movement should be free, strong and close. The hocks should be freely flexed and drawn close in under the body, so that when moving off the foot the body is thrown or pushed forward with some force. Stiff stilty movement behind is very objectionable.

FAULTS.

No. 1. *Coat.*—Any silkiness, wave, or tendency to curl is a serious blemish, as is also an open coat, and any black, grey, or wheaten hairs.

No. 2. *Size.*—Any specimens under the minimum weight, or above the maximum weight are objectionable.

No. 3. *Eyes.*—Full or light coloured.

No. 4. *Ears.*—Round-pointed, drop, semi-erect, also ears too heavily covered with hair.

No. 5. *Muzzle.*—Either under or over shot and defective teeth.

SWAITES ISLAY, THE FOUNDATION OF
MRS. L. PORTMAN'S KENNEL.

MR. C. H. BATTEN'S TOWER MHORA AND TOWER RONA.